T0119909

WISHING YOU A
MERRY CHRISTMAS!

From *Mary Engelbreit's Color ME Christmas Coloring Book*

ALL THE HAPPINESS YOU CAN HANDLE...

MERRY CHRISTMAS AND HAPPY HOLIDAYS!

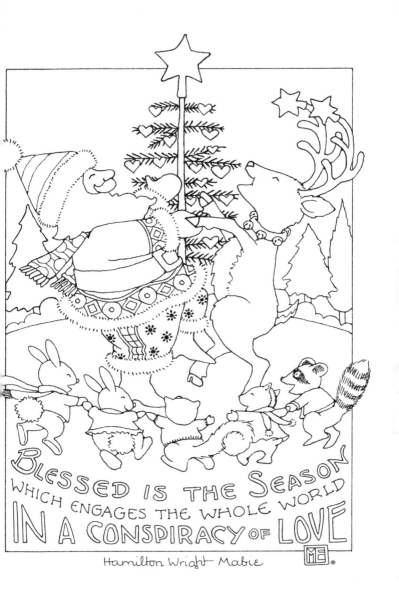

BLESSED IS THE SEASON
WHICH ENGAGES THE WHOLE WORLD
IN A CONSPIRACY OF LOVE

Hamilton Wright Mabie

A VERY MERRY CHRISTMAS TO YOU!

WISHING YOU A
MERRY CHRISTMAS!

JOY

MERRY CHRISTMAS

MERRY CHRISTMAS AND HAPPY HOLIDAYS!

A VERY MERRY
CHRISTMAS TO YOU!

WISHING YOU A
MERRY CHRISTMAS!

MERRY CHRISTMAS AND
HAPPY HOLIDAYS!

A VERY MERRY CHRISTMAS TO YOU!

E IS FOR

ELF.

WISHING YOU A

MERRY CHRISTMAS!

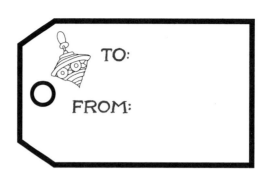

TO:

FROM:

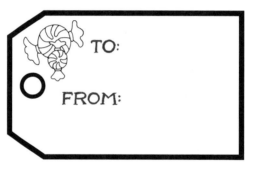

TO:

FROM:

TO:

FROM:

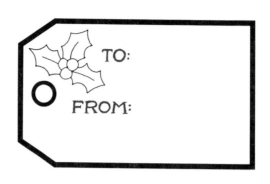

TO:

FROM:

TO:

FROM:

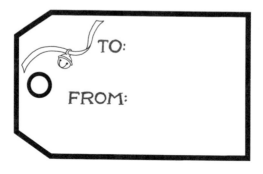

TO:

FROM:

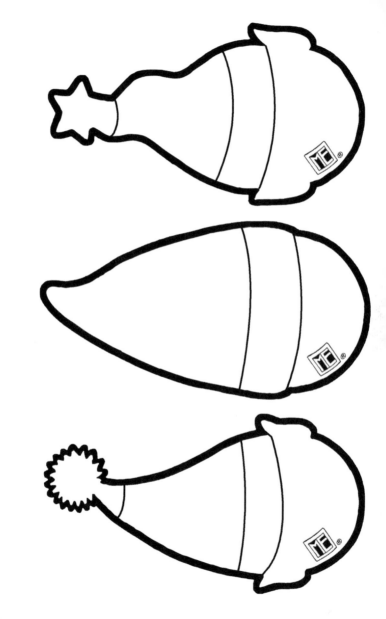

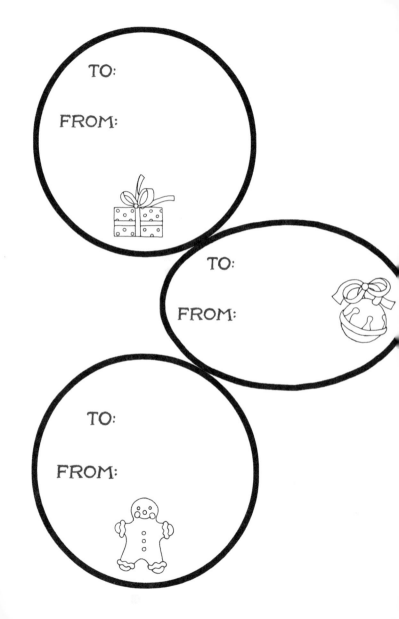

TO:

FROM:

TO:

FROM:

TO:

FROM:

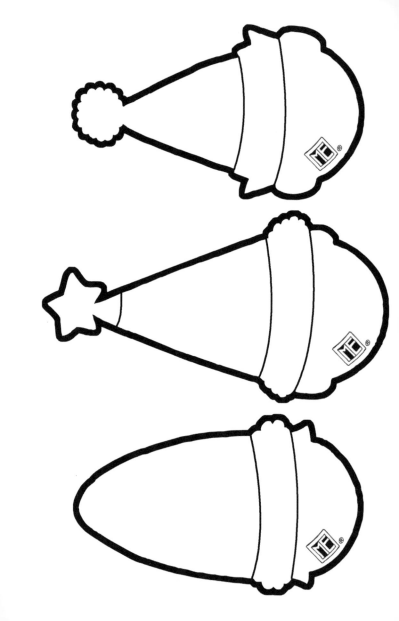

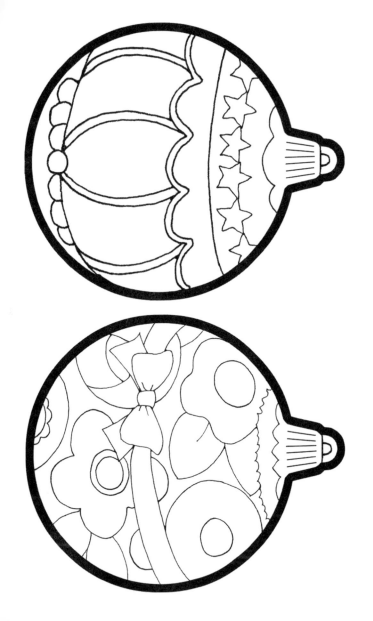

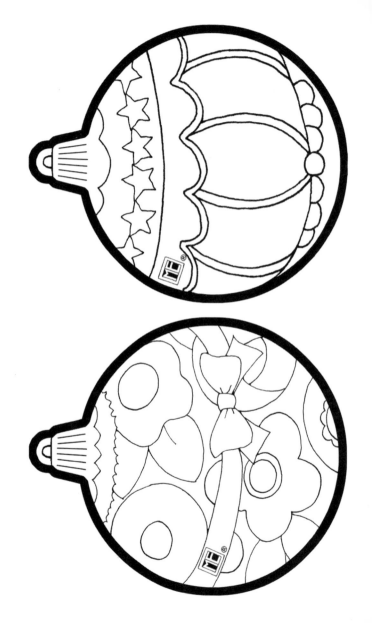

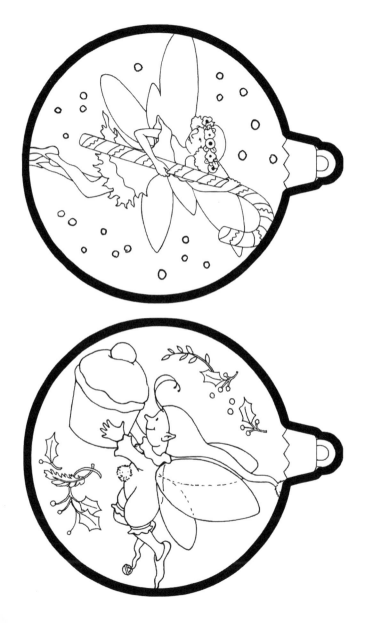

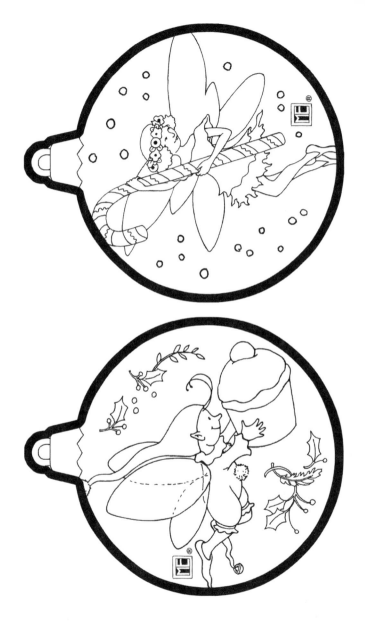

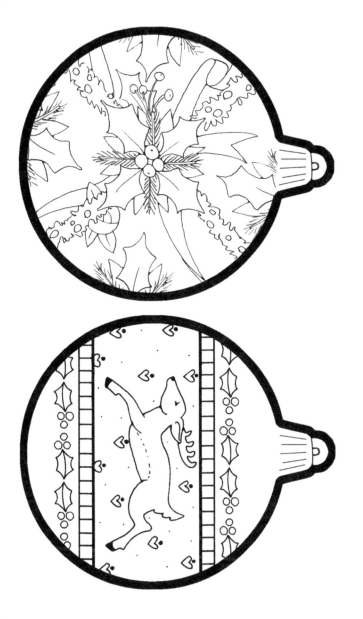

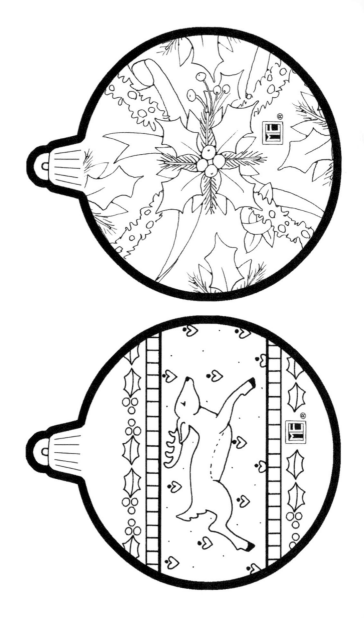

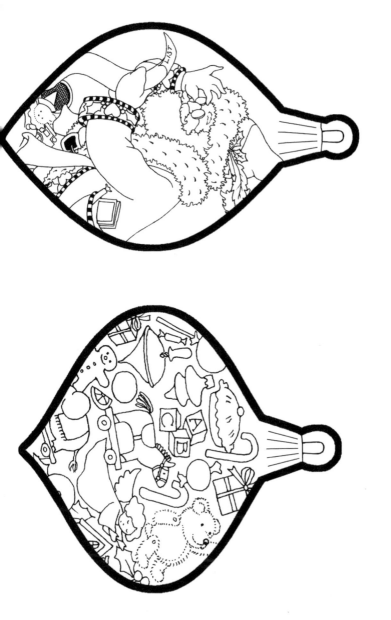

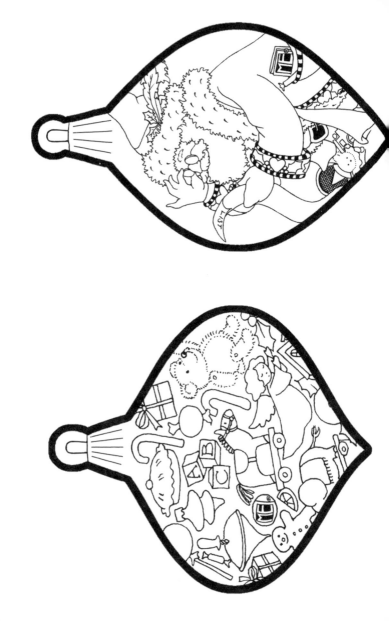

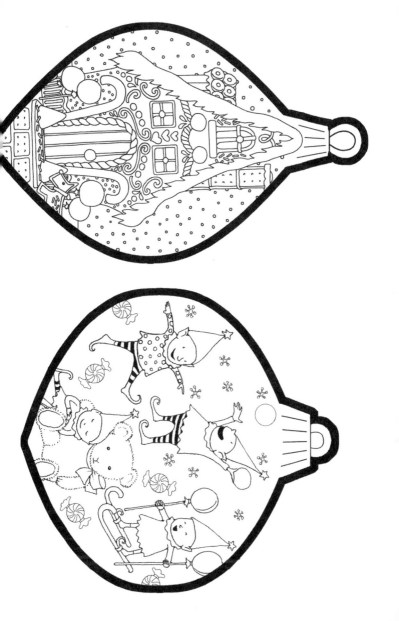

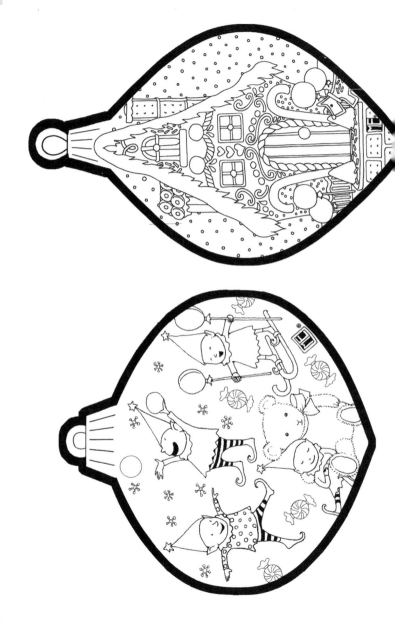